Keto Life

The Easy and Clarity Complete Guide to Daily Low Carb Meal Prep for Weight Loss, Fat Burning, and a Healthy Life for Simply Ketogenic Diet

Table of Contents

KETO LIFE 1

    TABLE OF CONTENTS_Toc62485907 6

INTRODUCTION 8

CHAPTER 1: THE BASICS OF KETO 10

    BAD BREATH 43
    DRY MOUTH AND EXTREME THIRST 44
    FATIGUE 46
    DIGESTIVE PAINS 48
    INCREASED HUNGER 51
    TROUBLE SLEEPING 54
    HEADACHES 56
    THE MACROS AND MICROS 58
    THE THREE MAIN TYPES OF THE KETO DIET 72

CHAPTER 2: HOW THE KETOGENIC DIET CAN HELP 92

    LOSE WEIGHT NATURALLY 96
    LOWER CHOLESTEROL 99
    REDUCE YOUR RISK OF CANCER AND POSSIBLY SHRINK TUMORS 102
    TREAT ALZHEIMER'S DISEASE 104
    RELIEVE THE SYMPTOMS OF MENTAL ILLNESS 107

Introduction

The ketogenic diet is taking the world by storm, yet many people are unaware of what it entails and how to begin. In this book, you will learn everything you need to know about the keto macro and micro ratios, the science behind the diet, how the diet can aid in weight loss, treating illness with ketosis, tips and tricks for losing weight, the best foods to enjoy and avoid, meal prepping, how to customize the keto diet and meal prepping to your lifestyle, and more! By the time you finish this book, you will feel confident in your ability to use keto not only to lose weight but also to gain health and energy. There is no need to buy a large stack of books to help get you on your way, as Keto Life contains all of the information you need to get started, feel well informed, and confident.

Upon first hearing about the ketogenic diet, many people are rightfully concerned that it may be a fad or a crash diet. While these diets often cause harm to peoples' health, ruin their metabolism, and cause weight loss stalls, this is not true of the ketogenic diet. In fact, the keto diet has been used for a century in the treatment of diseases and, more recently, for weight loss. While carbohydrates or carbs are by no means the enemy, excessive amounts can cause insulin resistance, diabetes, weight gain, and more. Yet, by greatly reducing the number of carbs you eat, you can enter into a state of ketosis, where your body is better fueled. This state will allow you to increase weight loss, energy levels, sleep better, and protect your brain from age-related diseases. But this is only the beginning. Throughout this book, you will learn all of the amazing benefits that this lifestyle has to offer.

Why hold yourself back? Take a step forward for increased health and a maintainable weight loss.

Chapter 1: The Basics of Keto

Practically every day, we hear about a fad or crash diet, whether it's Paleo or gluten-free, the cabbage soup diet, or the military diet. Some of these are healthier than others, whereas crash diets are obviously detrimental to health. Sadly, many people resort to these diets as they are unable to lose weight. However, all these diets do is cause damage to the body and metabolism, making you gain more weight than you had started with.

Thankfully, there are other options. You don't have to resort to the ineffective and harmful crash and fad diets. While the ketogenic diet has been gaining in popularity, unlike fad diets, it has a long history of scientifically-backed benefits. The ketogenic diet has been used for a century in the treatment of disease, and in this process, it has been studied extensively time and again. Not only has it been shown to effectively treat neurological and neurodegenerative diseases, but it has also been shown to increase maintainable weight loss, boost the metabolism, protect the brain and cells from damage, and heighten energy levels.

The groundwork for creating the ketogenic diet began in France in 1911. The purpose of the testing was to find a way of eating that could aid in the treatment of controlling seizures and epilepsy. However, simultaneously, there were studied ongoing in the United States by Dr. Hugh Conklin. This doctor found that by placing his epileptic patients on a twenty-five day fast, he could improve their symptoms and lessen seizure activity. Dr. Conklin's adolescent patients experienced relief, who had a ninety percent rate of success.

Soon thereafter, in 1916, Dr. H. Rawle Geyelin, a renowned endocrinologist working at the New York Presbyterian Hospital continued with studies similar to Dr. Conklin's. After the study was a success on his thirty-six patients, Dr. Geyelin presented the report to the American Medical Association. With this success, there was soon a surge of similar studies on epilepsy and diet.

This research was amazing and groundbreaking, not only for its time but to this very day. This research helped to change the treatment of epilepsy worldwide. Even at this point in time, it is still being used to treat patients who are resistant to drug treatment for their epilepsy. While long-term fasting is not a healthy option for treatment, this opened new doors for doctors to learn about ketones, ketosis, and how a low-carbohydrate and high-fat diet could result in the same benefits. Although, without the risks and difficulties that come along with long-term fasting.

Due to the earlier success, during the early 1920s, the study diet in relation to epilepsy continued to be studied. In fact, due to Dr. Conklin's earlier success, one of the parents of the children he had treated approached his brother with a deal. He would fund five-thousand dollars in research funds, which the brother would then use in his position as professor of pediatrics at Johns Hopkins Hospital.

Then Dr. Rollin Woodyatt, during the year 1921, made a major discovery that leads to the well-known success of the ketogenic diet. Not only did this discovery change the treatment of epilepsy, but the treatment of other diseases such as Alzheimer's and Parkinson's as well. Dr. Woodyatt was an endocrinologist, and he was the person who discovered ketones. These ketones are the very thing that gives the ketogenic diet its name. He found that these ketones are produced within the liver during a state of fasting, starvation, or when undergoing a low-carbohydrate and high-fat diet. These are water-soluble and come in three forms: acetone, acetoacetate, and beta-hydroxybutyrate. The discovery of ketones was a reason for high hopes within the medical community, for patients, and their families. Having discovered ketones, it was proven that people could maintain a beneficial way of eating long-term to treat their disease without needing to fast or becoming deficient in any vital nutrients.

This lead to Dr. Peterman of the Mayo Clinic soon thereafter using the ketogenic diet for the treatment of his patients with epilepsy. It was such a success that he urged the caregivers of his patients to learn how to help the patient follow the ketogenic diet after going home. Dr. Peterman would even help them learn how to customize the diet plan for each individual and communicate freely with the patients after they had gone home. During this time, his patients not only experienced a profound decrease in seizure activity, their cognitive function and behavior also improved.

Before long, the ketogenic diet was well-known within the medical community for its treatment of epilepsy. Study after study proving its safety and effectiveness was published in the following century. Between 1941 and 1980, nearly all of the textbooks covering childhood epilepsy explored the ketogenic diet and the success it offers.

However, the surge of the ketogenic diet did slow down for a time. Despite its success and popularity, it naturally went into a short decline when anticonvulsant drugs were discovered. Doctors naturally thought that anticonvulsants were the new answer to epilepsy treatment, and they began to be prescribed regularly. Yet, they would soon find that there are many people who are resistant to drug treatment. For these people who find little to no help with anticonvulsants, the ketogenic diet was an alternative treatment that offered much success without the long list of medication side effects.

Despite the decline in the use of the ketogenic diet, a doctor from the University of Chicago, Dr. Peter Huttenlocher, continued research on the subject. He was able to make a discovery of great benefit to people on the ketogenic diet and even people seeking an increase in ketones even without the diet. Dr. Huttenlocher found that medium-chain triglycerides, a type of fat that is highly concentrated in coconut oil and can be sold purely as MCT oil, is able to be transformed into ketones by the liver. This means that these medium-chain triglycerides, a shorter fat molecule that is in most foods, are able to further increase the ketones provided by the ketogenic diet. The benefit of this is that patients were able to slightly increase the number of carbohydrates they were consuming in their diet, without affecting the state of ketosis and whether or not the ketones were affecting their brains. Because of this, the ketogenic diet became more palatable and easier to follow.

Yet, despite Dr. Huttenlocher's efforts and the efforts of a few other doctors who saw the need for the ketogenic diet, its use continued to decline due to the use of anticonvulsants. Due to the decline, a great deal of misinformation about the ketogenic diet's effectiveness and safety soon spread.

Thankfully, the ketogenic diet once again made a resurgence in October of 1994. At this time, Dateline, a TV series on NBC, released an episode about epilepsy and the ketogenic diet. This episode focused on Charlie Abrahams and his family. While he was only two-years-old, Charlie experienced severe epileptic seizures. Despite trying anticonvulsant drugs one after another, his epilepsy refused to be reined in. But Charlie's parents refused to give up, and they poured over medical research themselves to look for an answer that Charlie's doctors hadn't considered. Before long, they found the research on the ketogenic diet and how it can effectively be used long-term in the treatment of epilepsy.

While his parents found what they believed to be the answer, most hospitals at the time refused to treat patients with the ketogenic diet. The doctors had come to believe that the keto diet was an inferior form of treatment when compared to anticonvulsant drugs. Yet, there was still one hospital continuing in the important research of the ketogenic diet. Charlie's parents soon took him to Johns Hopkins Hospital, where he saw an expert in the field, Dr. John Freeman. Although Charlie had found no success on a range of anticoagulant drugs, he soon made a remarkable recovery. With the ketogenic diet, Charlie's seizures, which had been causing delayed development, became under control. This allowed him to live life as a normal child his age and begin to catch up on developmental progress.

After the success of Charlie's treatment, his father, Jim Abrahams, created the Charlie Foundation. The purpose of this foundation is to fund further research, as well as to increase the visibility of the ketogenic diet for epilepsy and to help parents better advocate for their children. To further this goal, Jim Abrahams soon thereafter created a movie titled 'First Do No Harm,' telling their story and starring the multi-award-winning Meryl Streep as Charlie's mother.

The ketogenic diet once again received a renewed interest in 1998, especially in the medical community. Shortly prior to this, the American Epilepsy Society had conducted the first of its kind multicentre prospective study on the ketogenic diet. Once the results were published, the medical community finally realized that the ketogenic diet is a wonderful choice for people who are unresponsive to anticoagulants or who would prefer to avoid drug therapy and its inherent side effects.

The ketogenic diet has a long and robust history; it is clear to see that it is not some fad with false reports of success. The results of this lifestyle are plain to see and scientifically documented. Not only has it been shown to help epilepsy, but for the past two decades, it has been shown in study after study to help with obesity, weight loss, diabetes, insulin resistance, cancer, Alzheimer's disease, and more.

In order to understand why and how the ketogenic diet is able to have such profound effects, you first need to understand the process of ketosis and the mitochondrial cells within our bodies.

While every living organism is full of cells, we largely don't consider our cells, their health, and how they affect our biology. But these cells, especially the mitochondrial cells, are vital and interconnected to the ketogenic diet and how it affects our mind and body. It's important to understand that despite our cells being microscopic, they contain within them even smaller components. One of these components found within certain cells is the mitochondria.

The mitochondria within the cells provide them with a powerful ability to promote the body's health and survival. It does this because the mitochondria have a unique ability to convert more than one type of food source into energy. Rather than only converting carbohydrates, the mitochondrial cells are able to convert protein, fats, and carbohydrates into a fuel source for the body. In fact, these cells provide both humans and animals, with ninety percent of the energy we require to live. We couldn't survive without these powerful cells! If that weren't enough, these cells even produce vital chemicals, rid us of harmful toxins and oxidants, and recycle waste.

Although the mitochondrial cells may be able to use fat, protein, and carbohydrates as a fuel source, they will always first prioritize the use of carbohydrates. But there can be difficulties with this due to the large amount of carbohydrates found in many modern diets. Any time we eat grains, potatoes, dairy, sugar, or other sources of carbohydrates, then the mitochondrial cells will focus on only converting the carbohydrates found within those foods into the fuel. They will completely ignore the protein and fat, which we also require for fuel.

This prioritization is for multiple reasons. Firstly, because carbohydrates turn into glucose after being consumed, which is a quicker source of energy than either fat or protein. This means that by prioritizing carbohydrates, the mitochondrial cells can ensure that the body receives energy more quickly.

Secondly, when digesting excessive amounts of fuel, the body will store it for use later on. For instance, as body fat. But carbohydrates, after being converted into glucose, can only be stored in limited amounts. Within our liver and muscles, we can have an average of two-thousand calories worth of glucose at one time. Having the glucose within our muscles and liver in this way enables us to use it quickly when we begin to run or another form of exertion on short-notice. Any remainder glucose that is unable to be stored is then converted into lipids to be stored as body fat. Because of this, the mitochondrial cells try to save the body energy by prioritizing the glucose over the other fuels so that it doesn't have to be converted into fat to be stored.

The problem with this is that glucose is not a very effective fuel source, and we don't even require dietary sources of glucose. On the other hand, fats are essential to the human body and are more effective and efficient when used as an energy source when compared to glucose.

We may not be able to digest fats or convert them into an energy source as quickly as glucose; there are some fats that can be used more quickly. These fats are the previously mentioned medium-chain triglycerides found in coconut and MCT oil. Whereas most fat is found in the form of long-chain triglycerides, which require a longer digestion process, MCTs are already broken down and can, therefore, be utilized by the liver for fuel more quickly. This means that despite most fat not being as quick of an energy source as glucose is, there are still ways in which we can rectify this.

Thankfully, it is often unnecessary to have a quick source of energy on the ketogenic diet, even though MCTs can be helpful. This is because fats can be used as fuel for much longer than glucose. While glucose causes insulin and blood sugar spikes and crashes, resulting in the need to replenish, fat does not. Instead, fat offers us a sustained source of fuel that can keep us energized and satisfied for long periods of time.

The third of the fuel sources is protein. While most people only think of meat, dairy products, and eggs as offering protein, there are many plant-based sources that provide this fuel source as well. This source of fuel is one of the most vital because after being digested, protein is converted into amino acids. This is used not only to energize our bodies but to support our muscles and repair cells.

On the ketogenic diet, carbohydrates are naturally restricted, and we rely on high levels of fat and moderate levels of protein. Due to this, we push the mitochondrial cells into using a more effective source of fuel: fat and ketones. But we didn't mention ketones in the list of three fuel sources (fat, protein, and carbohydrates) so, what are they? Simply put, they are a new form of fuel that the body is able to create under specific conditions, such as on this diet.

The body creates ketones because there are certain cells that are unable to utilize fat as a fuel source. These cells are certain brain cells, red blood cells, testicle cells, and kidney medulla. These cells can survive through a process known as gluconeogenesis, in which the body converts amino acids such as dietary protein into glucose to be used specifically for the cells which require it. This is the reason why we are able to fully survive without glucose because our body is able to create it as long as we consume enough protein. Although, if we don't eat adequate levels of protein, then our bodies will begin to convert lean muscle mass into amino acids to be used in the gluconeogenesis process. For this reason, it is important to be sure to consume the appropriate levels of protein for your body, which we will explain in more detail later on.

Some people may be concerned the gluconeogenesis process could interfere with ketosis. After all, the body is creating more glucose. Due to this concern, there have been many people spreading the misinformation that you have to be careful not to consume too much protein on the ketogenic diet. This has been found to be inaccurate, as no matter how much protein we consume on the ketogenic diet, the gluconeogenesis process will not convert any more amino acids into glucose than it is required to in order to survive.

Ketones, also known as ketone bodies, come in three types: beta-hydroxybutyrate, acetoacetate, and acetone. These are produced by the liver whenever we are on a low-carbohydrate diet when fasting or consuming medium-chain triglycerides such as coconut oil. One of the many benefits of producing ketones is that it requires the body to rely less on the gluconeogenesis process. By doing this, the body is able to convert five times fewer amino acids into glucose than it otherwise would require. This is all in thanks to ketones having the ability to frequently be used by cells that are unable to utilize fat for fuel.

The reason that ketones are so effective in treating epilepsy and other brain-related diseases lies in the fact that it's a cleaner source of fuel. Just as carbon emissions can cause harm to the atmosphere, so too does glucose as a fuel cause harm to our brain. This is because while the brain may need a fast-acting source of fuel, glucose creates the most harmful type of oxidants when utilized, known as reactive oxygen species. These are the very same oxidants that are known to cause cellular damage and even cancer.

On the ketogenic diet, we are able to avoid a large portion of this damage caused by glucose since seventy-five percent of our brain cells are able to use ketones for fuel instead. This not only reduces the amount of damage the cells receive but can proactively protect the cells as well.

While these benefits are well enough on there own, there are even more reasons why we should use ketones as a fuel source:

•   While inflammation is an important part of the immune system, due to our diets, environment, and disease, many people have developed chronically high levels of inflammation. This inflammation causes a large number of problems, including an increased rate of mortality. Yet, ketones can directly lower levels of inflammation, including inflammation found in the brain. This specifically helps people with neurological or autoimmune diseases.

• In order to use fuel sources such as fat, protein, carbohydrates, and ketones, our body requires oxygen. While some of these fuel sources, such as glucose, require larger amounts of oxygen, ketones are able to be effectively used with a much smaller amount. This is beneficial as it increases our mental clarity, mental energy and even lowers the rate at which the brain ages.

• After being on the ketogenic diet for a time or in a prolonged state of ketosis, our body will naturally produce an increased number of mitochondrial cells within the brain. These cells will even become more effective. This is helpful since it enables more of the brain to be fueled by either fat or ketones rather than glucose.

• Most of our brain's neurons are formed prior to our birth, but there are some portions of the brain, which can use stem cells in order to produce younger and healthier cells. By using ketones as a fuel source, we are able to further the production of healthy neurons in the process known as neurogenesis. This is potentially life-changing for people with neurological and neurodegenerative diseases, as it increases the growth of neurons and synapses in the cortex, forebrain, hippocampus, as well as other areas of our brains.

• Glutamate is important for learning, the formation of memories, communication, and neural function. However, some people may develop an excess of glutamate, which causes damage leading to neurodegenerative diseases such as Alzheimer's disease, Parkinson's disease, multiple sclerosis, and Lou Gehrig's disease. Although with the use of ketones, our body is able to naturally keep our glutamate levels balanced to attain optimal brain health and potentially lessen the degeneration of these diseases or the diseases themselves altogether.

While you now understand how vital these ketones are, it's helpful to know how they are produced. Otherwise, you can easily make mistakes on the ketogenic diet that would prevent you from being able to produce ketones. Thankfully, as long as you have a general understanding of how the ketogenic diet and ketones work, then you should easily be able to maintain the diet and a state of ketosis.

In order to produce these ketones, we first have to use up the two-thousand calories worth of glucose that we have stored in our liver at any single point in time. This means that it may take some people a day or two to begin to create ketones, whereas people with insulin resistance may take up to a full week. Afterward, the fat we have eaten can be released into the bloodstream and used as a fuel source. During this process, many of the molecules are broken down in the beta-oxidation process into acetyl-CoA. The purpose of this process is to enable the cells that are unable to utilize fat to still gain fuel, such as that provided by ketones. Afterward, the molecules are once again transformed. They are turned into citrate, which can then be converted lastly into either ketone, ATP, or GTP for fuel as needed.

You will often hear of ketones being referred to as 'ketone bodies,' but this is not fully accurate as scientifically, they don't meet the needed requirements to be classified as a body. There is more than one type of ketones; these are beta-hydroxybutyrate, acetoacetate, and acetone, all of which are water-soluble.

After production, the ketones are released into the bloodstream to be used as fuel for the mitochondrial cells to turn into energy. While fat is unable to fuel the brain as it isn't able to go through the blood-brain barrier, ketones do not have this restriction. This means that they can fuel our brain and nervous system, all while protecting the health of our neurons. The protection that ketones offer to these neurons not only protects against neurological diseases, but it can even help reduce the damage of traumatic brain injuries and increase the healing after the injuries have occurred.

The reason that some people take longer to enter into a state of ketosis where their body is regularly producing ketones and using them as fuel is all because of glucose. Once we have glucose stored within our muscles and liver, it is known as glycogen, but everyone will burn through this amount of glycogen at different speeds. People who ate a relatively low number of carbohydrates and that are healthy or active will enter ketosis much more quickly than others, in as little as a day. However, the average person can expect it to take two to three days. On the other hand, people who consume a lot of sugar and carbohydrates, have insulin resistance, or diabetes will take longer than the average person to enter ketosis. For these people, it can take a week, even up to a week and a half, to burn through their stored glycogen and enter ketosis.

Thankfully, the ketogenic diet has been shown time and again to manage and treat both diabetes and insulin resistance. This means that the longer you are on the ketogenic diet, the more you can expect these conditions to improve.

How do you know if you are in ketosis? You can test for ketones with breath, urine, and blood samples. The most accurate form of testing is blood sampling, but urine strips and breath analyzers are the most readily available options.

But if using these two methods, you must keep in mind that they are not fully accurate because they only test for the excess ketones that the body is excreting. Over time, as you are on the ketogenic diet longer, your body will begin to make the correct number of ketones you require, and therefore, will not need to dump any excessive ketones. This can make it seem that you are no longer in ketosis, but it is actually a good sign. If you want a definite test for measuring ketone levels, then blood testing is the most accurate option but often is not needed.

Many people experience something known as the 'keto flu' at the beginning of the ketogenic diet. This is when people develop flu-like symptoms while their body is transitioning from being fueled by carbohydrates to fat and ketones. While the keto flu may not be pleasant, some people notice minimal to no side effects. Although, if you are one of the people who comes down with flu-like symptoms, there are ways you can manage them.

The way that these flu-like symptoms affect people differs from person to person. Yet, we have an idea of the most common symptoms and their causes. This makes it easier to avoid headaches and fatigue, as most of the symptoms have simple to treat causes such as dehydration.

People often experience little to no side effects during the first day or two of the ketogenic diet. However, some people might experience their regular food cravings and a slight increase in hunger. Don't worry; this hunger won't last. It is normal since you are used to eating a quick fuel source and are switching to a slow fuel source. Thankfully, you will notice within a couple of weeks that your hunger is diminishing, and after a month on the ketogenic diet, most people notice a significant decrease in hunger. During this time of increased hunger, you can simply include a couple of keto-approved snacks throughout the day to keep your energy levels up.

Most people experience most of the keto flu symptoms between day three and seven after starting the diet. This includes symptoms such as headaches, increased urination, muscle cramps, bad breath, digestive pains, dry mouth, increased heart rate or a pounding heart, increased thirst, insomnia, and fatigue. Again, most of these symptoms are caused by simple to fix problems, which we will go over in more detail in a moment.

After the first week, and during the second week, you will experience an increase in bad breath. This is because the ketone acetone is not very effective, but it is formed before the more effective acetoacetate and beta-hydroxybutyrate. For this reason, the body begins to dump acetone as it replaces it with more effective ketones. It dumps the acetone both through the breath and the urine, which is what both breath analyzers and urine strips tests are for. By the end of the second week, your breath should return to normal, and you will be in a sustained form of true ketosis.

By the beginning of either the third or fourth week, your energy should be increasing while your hunger decreases. Any other remaining symptoms of the keto flu should be lessening by the day. If you struggle with health issues such as insulin resistance or high cholesterol, then you may begin to see improvements in those issues at this point in time as well.

Bad Breath

We all dread bad breath, but you may have to live with it for a day or two of the ketogenic diet. This is because your body begins to produce ketones, and one of these ketones is acetone. Yet, our cells are unable to utilize acetone, so instead, it is excreted through both the breath and urine. This 'keto breath' may be rather pungent, smelling similarly to nail polish remover or overripe fruit. It is not pleasant.

Thankfully, it does not last long. Your body will quickly become acclimated to creating ketones and will produce the more productive ketones, beta-hydroxybutyrate and acetoacetate instead, and once it does, you will be in ketosis. There is not much you can do about the bad breath; just try to keep your distance from people and a lot of mints on hand for a couple of days.

Dry Mouth and Extreme Thirst

Due to restricting carbohydrates, your body will dump water weight and electrolytes rapidly. This will often cause dehydration, dry mouth, and thirst. While this is a good sign that the ketogenic diet is working for you, be sure you replenish fluids and electrolytes. You don't want to allow the dehydration to get out of hand.

It is most commonly recommended to drink half of your body's weight in ounces. Therefore, if you weigh one-hundred and fifty pounds, you will want to drink a minimum of seventy-five ounces of water a day. Although, more water than this would be ideal to ensure you are getting enough while your body is dumping a lot of its stored water.

Just be sure to never drink more than a liter in the time span of an hour, as your liver is unable to process more, and it would put a strain on your organs. Also, be careful to get the important electrolytes (sodium, magnesium, potassium, and calcium) along with the water, as the electrolyte molecules bind to the water molecules. This means that when water is dumped from your body, so are the electrolytes, and they need to be restored.

Now that you know about the overview of the keto flu, let's have a look at some of the most common symptoms, their causes, and how to combat them to make the entire process easier.

Fatigue

For the people who are hoping that the ketogenic diet will help relieve them of their chronic fatigue, hearing that the keto flu can cause further fatigue can be disheartening. But please do not fear. While the keto flu may cause increased fatigue in the short-term, in the long-term, the ketogenic diet has been known to greatly relieve people of chronic fatigue. Many people, after being on the diet for a few weeks, are amazed by how much more energy they have.

If you are experiencing increased fatigue from the keto flu, then you can most likely improve your symptoms by increasing your water and electrolyte intake, eating as frequently as needed, completing small amounts of light to moderate exercise, sleeping well, and eating enough protein throughout the day.

Digestive Pains

Most people are used to eating minimal to only a moderate number of fat and a large number of carbohydrates within their diet. Because of the change on the ketogenic diet, having digestive upset and pains isn't uncommon. Thankfully, for most people, these symptoms will pass, and their digestive health can even improve!

One of the most common digestive-related symptoms is diarrhea. This can be caused by multiple factors. Firstly, carbohydrates naturally bond to water molecules in our bodies. When we go on a low-carbohydrate diet, our body will naturally rid itself of these carbohydrates, but in the process, it will also dump many water molecules. This naturally causes diarrhea. Another common cause is the high-fat content. Since most people are unaccustomed to eating a high-fat diet, it can take time for their digestive system to properly process the increase in fat. Thankfully, over time, the body will begin to create more of the digestive enzymes and gastric juices it needs in order to digest fat. In the process, this will lessen stomach pains and diarrhea.

In the meantime, you can lessen the amount of coconut oil and MCT oil you are consuming. Since these two oils are digested much more quickly than other oils, it can cause an increase in diarrhea for people who are not yet accustomed to a high-fat diet.

While less common than diarrhea, some people may develop constipation. Thankfully, the ketogenic diet is known to resolve constipation, so as long as you follow the tips here, your constipation should ease. A large reason why people develop this constipation is that in order to remain on a low-carbohydrate diet, they greatly decrease their vegetable and fiber intake. However, both the nutrients in the vegetables as well as the fiber are essential to our health. While dairy and nuts might be allowed and enjoyed on the ketogenic diet, don't prioritize those ingredients over vegetables. Your first priority should be to consume all of the protein and vegetables you need; after that, you can enjoy products such as dairy, nuts, and seeds. There are plenty of low-carbohydrate vegetable options such as broccoli, spaghetti squash, asparagus, and more.

Another common cause for this constipation is dehydration. As we mentioned, when we go on a low-carbohydrate diet, it causes our body to dump many water molecules that had been bound to carbohydrates within our bodies. Because of this, we can easily become dehydrated. In the process, dehydration causes constipation. Ensure that you are consuming ample amounts of water and electrolytes in order to resolve this. You can't only drink water without refueling on electrolytes; otherwise, you will make your dehydration worse. Therefore, try to either enjoy foods that are high in the electrolytes sodium, potassium, magnesium, and calcium, take an electrolyte supplement, or drink keto-approved electrolyte drinks such as Ultima Replenisher.

Digestive upset and pains are some of the most common side effects of the keto flu. But if you follow these tips, then you can either avoid these problems or greatly lessen them. If you stick to the ketogenic diet, then these issues should resolve within a matter of a few weeks, and your digestive health may become even better than before.

Increased Hunger

People often experience increased hunger during their first few weeks of the ketogenic diet. This can be annoying and frustrating, especially since this is the period in which you are most likely to experience food cravings. This can especially frustrate people who are hoping to lose weight, knowing that fat is more calorie-dense than carbohydrates. But while you adjust to the ketogenic diet and your body learns to process the fats instead of carbohydrates, you may want to increase your calories to a maintaining-weight calorie count rather than a weight-loss calorie count. This can help lessen stress and hunger, and in the process, prevent you from overeating and gaining weight.

It is all too common for people to avoid eating, even when desperately hungry, because they want to avoid gaining weight or want to increase weight loss. The only problem is that this almost always causes a person to overeat later on, only worsening the problem. Instead, try listening to your body and eating a keto snack when you are hungry or low on energy. Don't worry; this phase won't last.

Over time, you will notice that you naturally feel less hungry. This is due to fats being a much more satisfying and longer fueling food than carbohydrates, which causes blood sugar crashes and intense hunger pangs. While you may need to eat more frequently within the first month of being on the ketogenic diet, you should find that afterward; you are able to eat less and go long periods without eating. Although, you are doing this while still eating all of the nutrients your body requires if you are following the ketogenic diet, as explained in this book.

The ketogenic diet isn't about restricting calories or eating less, rather listening to your body and its natural needs. You are simply able to eat less because fats are more satisfying than carbohydrates and higher in calories. By enjoying fats, you will be losing weight while fully supplying your body with healthy fuel, and without limiting your nutrient intake.

Trouble Sleeping

There are many people around the globe who suffer from insomnia, which is either the ability to fall asleep or stay asleep. This is problematic because it limits what they can accomplish in a day and affects their overall health. Some people, upon beginning the ketogenic diet, will find that they begin to experience insomnia, even if they had no previous experience with this condition. While this symptom is troubling and problematic, thankfully, it is usually short-lived and will go away with the other symptoms of the keto flu within a week or two.

The reason for the insomnia is simple, and thankfully, that also means that the solution is simple. The solution is so simple, in fact, that most people only have to wait a bit of time, and insomnia will resolve itself. The cause of this insomnia is that while the body is attempting to adjust to using fat as fuel rather than carbohydrates, an increase in stress hormone will naturally increase. These stress hormones, the most common being cortisol, are known to trigger insomnia. Thankfully, as your body adjusts to the new fuel source, the stress hormone should dissipate, and with that, insomnia should lessen.

While you wait for insomnia to resolve, there are a few solutions that may improve your sleep. Firstly, cardio exercises are known to increase stress hormones, so try to keep these exercises to a minimum.

On the other hand, yoga, meditation, and deep breathing are all known to lessen stress hormones and improve sleep. You can practice these throughout the day, but try to especially use these directly before bed to increase your sleep. Lastly, you can try to use over the counter sleeping aids, milk, or melatonin sleep aids, and generally, decrease stress within your day-to-day life.

Insomnia may be difficult to deal with, especially if we have a job, school, or kids to care for, but you will find that it soon improves, and you should feel better than ever!

Headaches

One of the most common symptoms of the keto flu is headaches and even migraines for some people. Thankfully, this is easy to resolve. This symptom is almost always caused by dehydration and an imbalance of electrolytes.

In order to resolve this imbalance, be sure to consume a minimum of half of your body's weight in pounds in ounces. This means that if you weigh two hundred pounds, you will need to consume one hundred ounces of water a day. If you only weigh one hundred pounds, then similarly, you would drink a minimum of fifty ounces. You can always drink more than this if you continue to experience headaches, but be sure to never drink more than a liter of fluids within the span of one hour. The liver is unable to process more fluid than that within an hour, and it can cause serious harm and risk to your body.

Along with water, you need to consume ample electrolytes. As previously mentioned, there is a keto-approved electrolyte drink, Ultima Replenisher. You can use this to increase your electrolyte levels, or you could even take electrolyte supplements. If you want to get these naturally in your diet, then look for low-carbohydrate vegetables, berries, nuts, and seeds that contain sodium, potassium, calcium, and magnesium. The amount of these electrolytes that a human needs vary from person to person, so be sure to check the government's recommendation based on your body weight, age, and gender.

The Macros and Micros

You know that you need a low-carbohydrate diet, but what exactly is considered low-carb? How much fat should you eat? How much protein do you need? Don't fear. In this portion, we will have all of the answers regarding carbohydrates, fats, and proteins, known as the macro ratio. Not only that, but you will also learn about your micronutrients such as vitamins and minerals.

If you've heard people talking about the ketogenic diet or perused some articles about it, then you've probably heard in passing the term 'macro ratio.' But since it's not a term most people use in their daily lives unless they're on keto, then it might be confusing to beginners. Yet, this is a necessary and extremely important aspect of the ketogenic diet. If you don't know about your macro ratio, you may cause your body confusion by constantly yo-yoing between being in ketosis and not in ketosis. You may even never reach ketosis if you are ignorant about the macro ratio because if you eat too many carbohydrates, you won't produce ketones. Not only that, but if you don't follow your macro ratio need for protein, then you could even begin to lose important lean muscle mass in the body.

Thankfully, by calculating an individual's macro ratio, we can determine exactly how much they should eat of the three main nutrients. This enables everyone to stay in ketosis, eat the proper amount of fat and enough protein.

Carbohydrates

On the ketogenic diet, most people aim to consume between twenty-five and thirty net grams of carbohydrates. When you read a food label, most of them offer total carbohydrate counts, not net carbohydrate counts. Thankfully, you can easily figure this out on your own. When calculating how many carbohydrates you are eating, simply remove the fiber count from the total carbohydrate count, and the remainder will be the net carbs. This means that if something has fifteen total carbs but ten grams of fiber, it is, in reallity, only five net carbs. The reason we do this is that the carbohydrates from fiber are not processed into glucose like other carbs; instead, they aid in our digestion to either bulk up or loosen our stools and to remove cholesterol.

Along with fiber, you also can generally remove sugar alcohols from the total carbohydrate count; this makes sodas that are sweetened with only stevia (an herb) and erythritol (a sugar alcohol) safe options on the ketogenic diet. This is because most sugar alcohols are not processed by the body but are instead dumped along with the fiber and waste. But it's important to keep in mind that because sugar alcohols are not fully digested that they may cause diarrhea or stomach pains in people with sensitive stomachs or if someone consumes a large quantity.

Thankfully, the most commonly used sugar alcohol at this point is erythritol, which is also the most gentle on the stomach. Many people are able to use this natural and sugar-free sweetener without negative side effects. While maltitol is no longer very common, be wary of anything containing this type of sugar alcohol. Most sugar alcohols are not fully digested, but maltitol is partially digested. This means that any foods containing this particular sugar alcohol will spike blood sugar and cause an insulin reaction, which you want to avoid on the ketogenic diet.

Carbohydrates are a wonderful source of all the macronutrients and even many micronutrients. They contain a large amount of protein and fat with a decent amount of fiber and carbohydrates. Although, they must be eaten in moderation because their net carb count quickly and easily adds up more than you would expect.

Some nuts, such as pistachios and cashews, are too high to be eaten on the ketogenic diet. Peanuts, which are not technically a nut, are eaten by some people and avoided by others. Ultimately they are a personal choice. Excellent choices of nuts if you want a pick-me-up or a flavoring option are almonds, macadamia nuts, and pecans.

Many people may avoid fruits and vegetables on the ketogenic diet. While you do need to be careful of the fruits you eat due to their natural sugar content, you can enjoy berries and even small amounts of melon in moderation. Similarly, it's important to consume a high quantity of vegetables daily. Try to aim for at least six to eight servings of low-carbohydrate vegetables. We will cover which vegetables are ideal options later on in this book, but there are plenty to choose from.

These are extremely important, partially for their fiber content. Fiber is incredibly important for human health. Without this compound, we would constantly be plagued by diarrhea or constipation. This is because there are two types of fiber—soluble and insoluble—and by having both, we are able to maintain ideal digestive health. Not only that, but fiber removes cholesterol and toxins from our bodies, making it vital to prevent and treat disease. Fiber even helps us better absorb the nutrients we eat it with so that we can make the most out of every food we are eating.

Whole grains and beans are high in fiber, but despite this, they are still too high in net carbohydrates to be included in the ketogenic diet. They would cause you to be thrown out of the state of ketosis, spike your blood sugar, and cause an insulin response. However, there is one exception: low-carb soybean products. Not all soybean products are made low in carbs, but those such as tofu are perfectly safe on the ketogenic diet. Some people choose to avoid soy completely. But it is a wonderful choice for vegetarian or vegan people who are looking to begin the ketogenic diet.

Again, the most commonly recommended number of net carbohydrates is twenty-five to thirty grams. Yet, some people who are highly active may bump that up to thirty to thirty-five. There are people who want to do a more hardcore keto diet in hopes of losing weight more quickly or preparing for an athletic competition. These people might eat as few as twelve net carbs a day.

But if you are only just beginning the ketogenic diet, I recommend staying at the standard twenty-five grams. You can always lower or raise slightly that number later on if you desire. Just be aware that if you raise it to the level of a highly active person and you don't exercise intensely and regularly, then you are unlikely to maintain a state of ketosis.

Fats

The main foundation of the three macronutrients on the ketogenic diet is healthy fat. While you will be eating a certain percentage of protein and most likely about twenty-five net carbohydrates, the remainder of the calories you eat within a day will come from your fat intake. The amount you eat is not specific but rather varies from person to person depending on their weight, activity level, and weight goals. Someone who is only one-hundred pounds and needs to put on weight will eat a higher calorie diet, meaning more fats. Similarly, someone who is highly active will burn through more calories and will also need more calories in fat than a person who is sedentary.

As an example of an average person, someone who is sedentary, five feet and five inches tall, weighs fifty pounds, and hopes to lose weight will most likely consume a diet of approximately twelve-hundred and eighty-two calories. This means that they need to eat one-hundred and one gram of fat, twenty-five net carbohydrates, and sixty-seven grams of protein. This can be adjusted to include either more or less fat if they want to increase their body weight or lose weight more quickly.

It is important to track all of your macro ratios, including fat. While eating the incorrect amount of fat won't disrupt the ketosis state, it will interfere with your weight goals. If you eat too little fat, then you won't have all of the calories your body needs to fuel itself. On the other hand, eating too much fat will quickly cause weight gain. It isn't difficult to accidentally eat several hundred extra calories worth of fat, which will cause your weight loss to stall.

Just because you can enjoy fat on the ketogenic diet doesn't mean you can enjoy any fat, though. There are many fats that are unhealthy and will only sabotage your long-term health. Instead, you should choose the healthiest options to include to also receive health benefits. This means you should avoid low-carb fried fast food, as it is made with unhealthy oils. The general rule of thumb is to avoid all trans fats and try to limit saturated fats to healthy sources such as coconut oil. Try to avoid vegetable oils such as those made from soy and corn. Many people loudly exclaim that all saturated fats are bad for you, but this simply is not true. Study after study has proven the health effects of coconut oil. It is a wonderful addition to your diet, especially in the treatment of disease and promotion of weight loss.

Better options for fats include those made from nuts, seeds, and fruits. This includes foods and oils such as avocados, olives, macadamia nuts, almonds, sunflower seeds, and sesame seeds. You can also enjoy butter, but if you can afford it, please choose a grass-fed option such as Kerrygold. Not only does this butter taste better, but it has an astonishingly higher number of nutrients than the typical grain-fed butter.

Proteins

When you first begin the ketogenic diet, you will need to calculate how much protein you should eat. Thankfully, this is made simple with online calculators such as the ones from Perfect Keto and Ruled.Me. These calculators will compare your height, weight, activity level, and weight loss goals in order to determine how many carbs, fats, and proteins you should be eating.

Despite the macro ratio being of such importance on the ketogenic diet, the biggest mistake people make is not tracking their macros. This can cause a stall in weight gain or even be detrimental if you are not consuming enough protein. Since there are some cells in our body that require glucose, the body will naturally create the glucose it needs out of amino acids. Ideally, it will get all of these amino acids from the protein we eat in our diet. But if someone eats too little protein, then the body will begin to destroy its own lean muscle mass in order to create glucose. This leads to muscle atrophy and general weakness. To prevent this, an average of twenty-five percent of your daily calories should be sourced from protein. When choosing protein, pick the best cuts that you can afford. If all you can afford is a regular whole chicken on sale, that's fine. But if you can afford pasture-raised, grass-fed, and antibiotic-free varieties of meat, this is the best choice. Similarly, when choosing fish, it is often best to choose wild-caught. Try to find fattier cuts of meat, such as dark meat for poultry. When choosing red meat, try to find higher fat ratios such as fifteen to twenty percent fat cuts. Fatty fish, such as salmon and sardines, are not only a wonderful source of fat but also for omega threes.

If you enjoy lean cuts of meat, then you can eat these with high-fat sauces or side dishes in order to balance out your meal. Of course, you can also eat eggs, dairy, and nuts. But be careful of the carbohydrate levels in both nuts and dairy.

In a nutshell, on the standard ketogenic diet, a person will eat an average of twenty-five grams of net carbohydrates, twenty to twenty-five percent of calories from protein, and the remainder of their calories should be from fat.

The Three Main Types of the Keto Diet

The Standard Keto Diet

Above, we mentioned the standard ketogenic diet and how it will look for an average person. But people can also follow the keto lifestyle if they are vegetarian, vegan, or dairy-free. It may take a little extra work to figure things out, but it is completely possible.

Although, these are not the types of the ketogenic diet we are discussing here. While the standard keto diet may be the most widely used and versatile, there are two other types that highly athletic people often follow. This isn't to say that you can't enjoy the standard ketogenic diet when you are highly active, but some people may benefit from one of the two other types more.

However, the other two types of keto diet do include an increased amount of carbohydrates. Therefore, if you are trying to get into a state of ketosis, it is recommended to follow the standard keto diet for a full month before trying one of the other two versions.

The Targeted Keto Diet

If you are athletic and don't feel that the standard ketogenic diet is quite enough to give you the energy you need, then the targeted keto diet is the most simple option to increase your energy and boost your performance. If you practice standard cardio, aerobics, yoga, or other light to mildly intense exercises, then you should be fine on the standard ketogenic diet. But, if you prefer highly intensive exercises such as high-intensity interval training (HIIT), heavy weightlifting, or high-intensity sports, then the targeted ketogenic diet may be the answer to your problems.

The targeted keto diet is also a wonderful option for people who only work out at irregular periods or less than three times a week. With this method, you can truly customize it to your individual needs, workout, and schedule.

Following this version of the diet is simple and straightforward. When you know you are going to have a high-intensity workout, simply enjoy a higher carbohydrate meal thirty minutes prior. This will be enough time for your body to convert the carbohydrates into glucose and glycogen and have them stored within your muscles and liver for quick-release energy. Somewhere between twenty-five to fifty net carbohydrates is ideal, as you don't want to eat too many or else you won't burn them off in the process of your exercise. With this amount, you can ensure you are properly energized but can still remain in ketosis.

When following this method, try to stick to healthy sources of carbohydrates, such as a very small serving of whole grains, beans, or fruit. However, some of the best options are sweet potatoes and beets. These two vegetables are bursting with nutrients which can further boost your workout.

It's important to keep in mind that while the twenty-five to fifty grams of net carbohydrates doesn't have to fit within your daily net carbohydrate count if you are attempting to lose weight, you will want them to fit within your calorie count. This means that if you eat fifty calories worth of carbohydrates, then you will want to remove fifty calories worth of fat from your diet for the day. This will ensure you are still maintaining your caloric goal.

The Cyclical Keto Diet

While the targeted keto diet is ideal for people who workouts at high intensities irregularly, the cyclical is a more complex version perfect for people who workouts regularly. While more complex, some people find this method really beneficial if they work out at high intensities an average of four to five days a week. Someone can not follow the cyclical keto diet if they work out less than this, because they will be unable to maintain ketosis.

The cyclical keto diet uses a schedule of high-carb and low-carb days to enable you to completely fuel your workout while still maintaining ketosis. Instead of only eating the carbohydrates directly prior to a workout, you will be enjoying a day or two on a high-carb diet before switching back to low-carb.

This method works best for people who can keep to a schedule and are able to burn off all of the carbohydrates that they are eating. The most-used schedule for the cyclical keto diet is as follows:

Day One

Five hours prior to a workout, begin to eat a high-carbohydrate meal. You can then eat an additional high-carb snack, about twenty-five to fifty net carbs worth, two hours before your workout. This enables your body to enter an anabolic state, which increases healing and promotes muscle building. For your snack, fruits that contain both fructose and glucose are a good choice, as this helps your liver and muscles be more prepared with glycogen before your workout.

Overall, you will want this first day's calories to be fifteen percent from protein, fifteen percent from fat, and seventy percent from carbohydrates.

Day Two

You want to lower your carbohydrate intake on the second day, but you will still be consuming a higher percentage than usual to finish off your carbohydrate load. Overall, you want sixty percent of your calories to be from carbs, twenty-five percent from protein, and fifteen percent from fat.

In order to prepare to begin burning off the carbohydrates and promote a state of ketosis, try to avoid eating anything after six in the evening. If you must get a snack, then choose something as low in carbohydrates as possible. By having a fast between dinner and breakfast the following day, you are beginning to start the process of burning off the glycogen.

It's always important to have rest days. Try to take the second day off of exercise, or at the very least, only perform mild exercise rather than intense. It may feel unproductive to rest, but this is an important part of the process as any trainer will tell you. By resting, you are not only reducing the likelihood of developing injuries, but you are also helping your muscles to grow back stronger and healthier.

Day Three

On this day, try to hold off on breakfast until after your intense workout. By exercising in a fasted state which is important on the cyclical keto diet, you will be able to burn off the glycogen stores. If you don't prefer to work out while fasting, then the targeted keto diet may be a better option for you. Try to consume no more than twelve net carbohydrates on this day.

Day Four

The fourth day should be a break from high-intensity, and instead, you can work on moderately intense exercises. You can begin to bump up your carb count on this day. Try to aim somewhere between fifteen and twenty net carbs.

Days Five and Six

You can now go up to twenty-five net carbohydrates on these days, as well as those following. Continue your high-intensity workouts in the mornings while fasted.

Day Seven

Allow yourself to eat as normal with twenty-five net carbs and rest on this day to recover from the previous two days and prepare for the next.

Day Eight

Workout in a fasted state as usual with a high-intensity workout. After day eight, repeat back to day one and continue with this cycle.

You now have an understanding of your macros, their importance, and how to fit them to your individual body, lifestyle, and weight loss goals. But now it is time to discuss something of equal importance, yet frequently forgotten about—the micronutrients.

While the biggest mistake on the keto diet may be not tracking the macro ratio, the second most common mistake is ignoring the micronutrients. This is why the ketogenic diet may sometimes get a bad rap. People assume that you are unable to get adequate nutrition while on the keto diet, but that is not true at all. You simply need to stay aware of nutrients and ensure that you are eating a balanced variety. This includes vitamins and minerals such as vitamin C, magnesium, D3, potassium, calcium, and more.

Many people assume you can only get these in fruits and vegetables, and while they are abundant in these foods and you will be getting them from these ingredients, there are other sources as well. In fact, meats, grass-fed butter, and eggs contain a surprising number of micronutrients.

Sodium

First, before we cover the other micronutrients, the most important to cover are the electrolytes. This includes sodium, magnesium, potassium, and calcium. Why are these the most important? Because when we go on a low-carb diet and lose the water molecules that were attached to the glucose within our bodies, we will also lose large amounts of electrolytes. While replenishing on water and staying hydrated is important, it is equally important to replenish your electrolytes. Without these micronutrients, our cells wouldn't be able to properly communicate, leading to a wide range of medically serious condition. A deficiency in electrolytes will greatly affect both our brain and heart, among other parts of our bodies.

Sodium or salt may have a bad reputation, and while we certainly don't want to eat too much of this nutrient, we can't forsake it altogether. It's important to remember that if you are no longer eating a diet high in processed foods, your sodium levels will be greatly reduced. Just as the other electrolytes are important for our cells communication, so too is sodium.

If you have insulin resistance, you may find that the longer you are on the ketogenic diet, the more likely you are to develop a sodium deficiency. This is because people with an unhealthy insulin response hold onto sodium. As they are on the keto diet, and their insulin response becomes healthier, they will naturally hold onto less sodium. People who are active or sweat frequently should be especially careful of electrolyte imbalances.

Some of the most common symptoms of sodium deficiency are fatigue, headaches, and weakness. You should especially watch for this during the beginning, two to three weeks on the keto diet. If you notice these symptoms, then you should be sure to include more electrolytes within your diet. The standard sodium intake recommendation is three to five grams on a daily basis.

Magnesium

One of the other electrolytes, magnesium affects over three-hundred of the body's biological functions. The most common side effects of magnesium deficiency are muscle cramps, fatigue, and dizziness. But this electrolyte can also affect anything from the synthesis of protein to our reproduction system. The recommended daily intake of magnesium is five-hundred milligrams. You can easily get this amount in electrolyte drinks, multivitamins, and your regular diet. Some of the best keto sources of magnesium include pumpkin seeds, Swiss chard, and oysters.

Potassium

When hearing about potassium, most people first think of bananas. Since bananas are too high in carbs to be eaten on the keto diet, this may concern some, but thankfully, there are plenty of other sources where you can get this vital nutrient. But if you are not being sure to consume adequate potassium levels, you could develop a deficiency leading to muscle loss, weakness, heart palpitations, irregular heartbeat, irritability, constipation, and skin disorders. This nutrient is so important that people who are severely deficient may develop heart failure.

Thankfully, you can easily consume the recommended forty-five hundred milligrams of potassium daily on the ketogenic diet. Some of the higher food sources include mushrooms, avocados, and kale.

Many people know that spinach is high in potassium, but it's actually recommended to avoid this for potassium intake. This is because spinach is also high in what is known as oxalates. These oxalates prevent your body from absorbing the nutrients that are consumed with it, meaning you will unlikely absorb any of the potassium in the spinach.

Calcium

The last of the electrolytes, calcium, is rather easy to consume enough of on the keto diet. However, if you are not consuming enough, then you can have irregular blood pressure, irregular clotting of the blood, weak bones and teeth, and again, the cells will be unable to properly communicate with one another.

It is recommended to consume between one and two grams of calcium a day, which many people on the keto diet get from low-carb dairy options. Although, if you don't care for dairy or are dairy-free, you can also get ample amount from bone-in sardines, bone-in canned salmon, cooked kale, raw broccoli, and almonds.

Iron

There are two types of iron, which is important to understand when you are trying to increase your intake. There is heme iron which is found in animal sources and non-heme, which is found in plant sources. This is important to understand because non-heme iron is not easily absorbed.

To increase absorption of iron, it is best to consume it throughout your meals rather in one large meal. This is because iron is most easily absorbed in small doses. You can also cook your food in cast iron cookware to increase your iron levels easily and naturally. By consuming vitamin C with your iron, you may be able to absorb five times more of it than you otherwise would.

It is best to avoid chocolate, coffee, and tea within two hours of consuming iron, as these ingredients contain compounds which are known to regularly block the absorption of iron.

The recommended dosage for non-menstruating adults is 8.7 milligrams. Adults who do menstruate require a higher intake to avoid anemia are recommended 14.8 milligrams per day. However, iron levels can vary from person to person based on their health and any hidden complications. It is best to discuss this with your doctor, who will be able to test your iron levels and know what is best for you as an individual.

Some great sources of iron include liver, meat, eggs, coconut milk, mushrooms, dark leafy greens, olives, nuts, and seeds.

Vitamin D3

We are not covering every vitamin and mineral in this book, only those that people are most likely to be deficient in. While people who are on the ketogenic diet are no more predisposed to a vitamin D deficiency than anyone else, we are mentioning it here because a large percent of the population is already deficient in what is referred to as the sunshine vitamin. In fact, over forty-one percent of American adults are deficient in this vitamin. This is largely due to our time indoors and the use of sunscreen.

This is detrimental as vitamin D3 is equally important for bone health as calcium. This vitamin is also essential for the functioning of our nerves and immune system. Being deficient in this vitamin increases your risk of depression, diabetes, heart disease, cancer, and autoimmune disease. Not only that, but this vitamin helps us to better absorb both calcium and phosphate.

You can greatly benefit your D3 by spending thirty minutes outdoors a day. However, sunscreen and clouds will block your absorption. You also don't want to increase your risk of sun cancer. Therefore, many doctors recommend their patients take a vitamin D3 supplement.

There are many other vitamins and minerals that people become deficient in. While we are unable to cover all of them in this book, it is important that you are receiving adequate levels of these micronutrients. Therefore, it is recommended to ask your doctor to run a complete blood panel on both your vitamins and minerals. With this panel, your doctor will know if you are getting either too much or not enough of any essential nutrients. Once you have this information, you can simply tailor your diet to your individual needs.

Chapter 2: How the Ketogenic Diet Can Help

Before getting into the benefits of the ketogenic diet and how it has been scientifically proven to help a number of conditions, let's first evaluate its safety. People occasionally raise concern over its safety, but in general, that is because they have not seen the research surrounding it. In fact, study after study has been conducted on the safety of the ketogenic diet, and each one has found it a viable and safe option.

Although, if you have a chronic illness or disease, please always check with your doctor before making large dietary changes.

One of the most common concerns people have is ketoacidosis. This concern is because it obviously sounds similar to ketosis, but the two states are quite different. While they both have ketones in common, one is a potentially life-threatening condition caused by diabetes, and the other is a perfectly safe and natural effect brought about by fasting or the ketogenic diet.

Ketoacidosis is caused when a person who has diabetes becomes deficient in insulin. This process is caused when the lack of insulin is unable to properly communicate with our cells. This causes some of our cells, specifically those in fat and liver, to enter starvation mode despite having eaten. As this progress, the fat cells which have been affected will release triglycerides into the bloodstream in an attempt to energize the body. These triglycerides go to the liver where they create ketones more quickly than the body is able to process. This soon causes ketones to build up in the bloodstream, high blood sugar, dehydration, and the blood soon turns acidic.

If you have diabetes and suspect you may be experiencing ketoacidosis, then please seek emergency medical attention right away. Thankfully, with proper care of diabetes, this condition is preventable. Some studies have even found that the ketogenic diet may help in the prevention of ketoacidosis. This is due to the diet helping to regulate blood sugar and insulin, preventing the initial cause of ketoacidosis. All diabetics should only begin the ketogenic diet under the close supervision of their doctor, and likewise, they shouldn't discontinue any medication without their doctor's approval and guidance. However, many studies have found that under their doctors' care, many diabetics have been able to discontinue or greatly reduce their medication on the ketogenic diet.

For people without diabetes, ketoacidosis is extremely uncommon, and there are no reports of it being caused by the ketogenic diet. In fact, if you enjoy a keto lifestyle, you may even prevent yourself from developing diabetes as you age.

While the ketogenic diet has been found safe, it is recommended against people who have kidney disease to attempt. Studies have not been conducted on its safety for those who are pregnant or breastfeeding, so they should avoid the diet without a doctor's direct approval.

Now that we have covered the safety of the ketogenic diet, there are many benefits we can go over. With nearly one-hundred years' worth of research studies conducted, many benefits of this diet have been discovered. Not only can it be used in weight loss and epilepsy treatment, but for a number of other illnesses as well. Following, we will explore some of its most common and scientifically-backed uses.

Lose Weight Naturally

Whether trying to lose ten pounds or a hundred, the ketogenic diet has been found to greatly improve weight loss, even in people who are unable to lose weight on any other diet. This is especially helpful because science has shown that a higher body fat percentage can increase the risk of disease. This does not mean that we should shame people for being fat or that they can't be both fat and healthy, but the risk of health complications is greatly reduced at a healthy body mass index.

Many people will try to crash and fad diets to no avail. If that weren't already frustrating enough, these diets often lead to increased weight gain and nutritional deficiencies. On the other hand, the ketogenic diet is not a crash diet, it's not a fad, it's scientifically backed, and it has been successfully used for a century. On this plan, you can lose weight at a maintainable speed, all without starving your body of nutrients or calories. If you go off the ketogenic plan for a time, you don't have to worry about losing all your progress as you do with the other diets. But you may have no interest in discontinuing the keto lifestyle because it is easily maintained and has a host of benefits.

But why does the ketogenic diet succeed when so many other diets fail? When you are on a standard diet high in carbs, your blood sugar and insulin are constantly in turmoil. You experience highs and then crashes, which cause you to need to eat more frequently and even overeat. Not only that, but this process prevents your body from burning the fat you have eaten, keeping it stored as body fat rather than using it for fuel. On the other hand, when you are on a low-carb diet, you are able to constantly burn not only the fat you are eating but also the body fat you have stored for this very use. This process naturally boosts your metabolism.

Doctors have long known that losing weight too quickly is unhealthy for your metabolism and liver. Thankfully, on the ketogenic diet, you are able to customize how quickly you lose weight depending on how much you are eating. If you want to lose weight at a maintainable pace, you simply eat a slight calorie deficit. If you find that you are losing more than three or four pounds a week, then you can increase your calorie count in order to lose at a healthier rate.

However, you will lose more weight during the first week or two of the ketogenic diet. During this time period, you will lose a lot of water weight, which can be between five and fifteen pounds. This is not dangerous to lose quickly as it is different from weight loss from fat. But be sure to stay well hydrated and consume your electrolytes.

You can also either gain weight on the ketogenic diet if you are underweight. While more people come to keto in hopes to lose weight, there are those who are looking to gain. If you are under one-hundred pounds, for instance, then the keto diet may help. All you have to do is calculate your macro ratio with a weight gaining calorie count. This may mean that you eat two-thousand calories a day, but it will depend on your individual characteristics and lifestyle.

Lower Cholesterol

High cholesterol is plaguing America and leading people to heart disease. While we may hear that fats are bad for us and clog our arteries, the truth is that all fats are not created equal. The healthy fats promoted on the ketogenic lifestyle, for instance, have been proven to help lower cholesterol. Not only that, but multiple studies on the ketogenic diet have proven that eating this way lowers bad cholesterol time and again. If that weren't enough, it also raises our good cholesterol and decreases our risk of developing heart disease.

In fact, no study has shown that the ketogenic diet raises bad cholesterol. While it may raise our good cholesterol, as the name suggests, this is a good thing. This type of cholesterol known as HDL cholesterol improves our digestion, increases vitamin absorption, manages hormones, and decreases bad cholesterol. This type of cholesterol poses absolutely no risks to our health and only provides us with benefits.

In a study on sixty-six obese patients with high cholesterol, the ketogenic diet was able to greatly help. These people not only lost weight, but they also were able to lower their bad cholesterol, lower blood glucose triglycerides, and increase good cholesterol. At the end of the study, the researchers deemed it a success and found the ketogenic diet to be a viable treatment option for high cholesterol, obesity, and heart disease.

Reduce Your Risk of Cancer and Possibly Shrink Tumors

As we have mentioned, nearly all of our cells are able to utilize ketones for fuel rather than glucose. However, this is not true of cancer or tumor cells, which require glucose in order to grow and survive. While these cells may possibly gain some glucose despite being on the ketogenic diet, in general, the keto diet has been found to be a great success for the treatment of cancer and non-cancerous tumors.
By replacing glucose with ketones and fat, you are able to effectively starve these dangerous cells. Certain studies have even found that within several days of beginning treatment on the ketogenic diet, people have experienced shrinkage in both cancerous and non-cancerous tumors.

If that weren't beneficial on its own, other studies have found that the keto diet greatly increases the effectiveness in chemotherapy, prevents the further growth of tumors, and decreases negative symptoms.

It is important to note that these people often noticed their tumors once again began to grow if they stopped the ketogenic diet. This shows that a long-term keto lifestyle is most likely needed for people with this condition.

Treat Alzheimer's Disease

The rate of Alzheimer's disease and other age-related diseases have been dramatically increasing over the decades. In fact, in America, Alzheimer's is the sixth leading cause of death, providing people with only four to eight years of life expectancy after diagnosis. There are currently an estimated forty-four million people worldwide battling this disease and dementia, and there are many who go undiagnosed. According to Alzheimer's Disease International, only one out of every four people around the globe will be diagnosed. Shockingly, between 2000 and 2014, Alzheimer's-related deaths increased by eighty-nine percent. It is estimated that between 2017 and 2025, the numbers of Alzheimer's cases will continue to rise by fourteen percent.

With these statistics, it is easy to see why finding treatment for and prevention of Alzheimer's is vital. This disease is only continuing to worsen, and we must find an answer. Thankfully, some studies have shown that the ketogenic diet may provide an answer in many cases.

Alzheimer's disease causes the neurons in our brains to develop insulin resistance. This process causes the neurons to then have difficulty absorbing glucose and starve of fuel. The reason this can be lessened with the ketogenic diet is that ketones are able to fuel these cells that would otherwise be starved. Since these cells are unable to be fueled with fat and are no longer able to absorb glucose, ketones are an ideal alternative. Not only that, but the ketogenic diet can treat and decrease insulin resistance, thereby helping the cells to better absorb glucose in the future.

As we have discussed, coconut oil and MCT oil both cause the liver to produce ketones. For this reason, in one study, a patient was given these two oils for a treatment period of twenty months. The patient was able to regain much functioning and greatly improved overall. They were able to better recall events, experienced an increase in mood, were better able to recall words, experienced an increase in social activities, a decrease in tremors, and their ability to walk even improved.

In the official Alzheimer's Disease Assessment Scale-Cognitive improved by six points. They were additionally able to improve fourteen points on the Activities of Daily Living scale. The entire time they were on the ketogenic diet, MRI scans proved that their brain experienced no decline in health. A study on a larger pool of participants with both Alzheimer's disease and other cognitive impairments found success as well. In this study, twenty participants were given either a placebo or an MCT oil drink in order to increase their ketone levels. While those on the placebo noticed no change, those on the MCT ketone drink improved significantly within ninety minutes of each dose.

Lastly, there was a study comparing the effects of both low-carb and high-carb diets on senior adults. Unlike those on the high-carb diet, those on the low-carbohydrate diet experienced great improvement. These individuals experienced improved fasting insulin, improved fasting glucose, increased weight loss, decreased weight in the stomach, and improved memory functioning. At the end of the study, the researchers concluded that all of these benefits were a result of the ketones produced on the low-carb diet.

Relieve the Symptoms of Mental Illness

Sadly, mental illness is greatly stigmatized, despite it also being incredibly prevalent. This results in a large population of people suffering going without needed medical care. In fact, fifty-six percent of the people living with one of these illnesses do not seek help. While those with a mental illness are most likely to be the victims of violent crimes, people often promote the lie that mentally ill people are the perpetrators of these crimes.

While more studies need to be done on the ketogenic diet and mental health, the evidence so far is optimistic. This is extremely encouraging as these illnesses interfere with daily life, often preventing people from succeeding in their profession and unable to maintain a stable social life.

Bipolar disorder is one of the most common mental illnesses, affecting an estimated five and a half million Americans. Yet, this illness is also difficult to treat and highly misunderstood. In one study, women who were diagnosed with type II bipolar disorder found a great improvement in their mood after beginning the ketogenic diet. This was especially promising, as both women in the study were not able to achieve much help on drug treatment options. These women continued to experience improvement for the two to three years that the study tracked.

Studies on humans with depression in relation to the ketogenic diet still need to be conducted. Despite the limited clinical evidence, many people have claimed that the ketogenic diet has improved their depression. This is further supported by animal studied on depression and ketosis. In one study on rats, it was found that the ketogenic diet was equally as successful in treating depression as antidepressants. After beginning the diet, the rats became more alert and mobile, and they were no longer showing other signs of being depressed. There was another similar study that found these results to be true as well.

Autism may not be a mental illness, but it does often come along with anxiety disorder, depression, mood disorders, and other difficulties. While there are not yet many studies showing the ketogenic diet and its effect on autism, the ones that are available suggest it could help the mental illnesses that often go hand in hand with the condition, and it may also decrease stress triggered by social situations.

CPSIA information can be obtained
at www.ICGtesting.com
Printed in the USA
BVHW092053190421
605311BV00002B/55